Palmistry ~
Palm Readings In Your Own Words

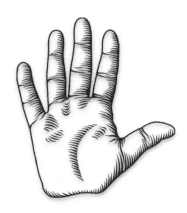

Julian Moore

Palmistry ~
Palm Readings In Your Own Words

Amazon Print Edition

To download the FREE audiobook of this text please
visit http://thecoldreadingcompany.co.uk
and look for the 'free audiobook' link

For the link to the ten flash cards that accompany this
text please see the back of the book

CONTENTS

FOREWORD

I've read many books on palmistry over the years, and although many of them go in depth in each chapter about different parts of the hand, I personally found them hard going as a novice palm reader. There was too MUCH information, presented in an order totally different to the way one would structure a palm reading.

One of the other problems I had when I was learning palmistry was that the books I was reading didn't explain very well how to relate the information found on the hand to the 'client' in a meaningful way. It's all very well knowing that someone has more 'logic' than 'willpower', but simply telling them that isn't very personal and could even be considered rather abstract! In this book I will explain how to connect the meanings on the hand to arrive at an interesting and useful reading.

This book and accompanying flash cards are designed for you to teach yourself the basics of palmistry as quickly as possible, structured so that with only a few cards memorized you can immediately start 'giving readings'. By having very simple and memorable information from the start, practicing on others can begin almost immediately, and as practice is the only way to become adept at palmistry, this is important. The cards are designed to be printed onto 4X6 index cards which you can get at any stationers.

The cards have names on the front and information on the back. This is so that you can test yourself and use the front of the cards to jog your memory of the order to do things. You will also notice on the front of each card is a small list. This is a further aid to remind you what is on the other side when you're testing yourself.

With the cards in your pocket or handbag, you have a quick and easy reference guide to refresh your memory before you do a reading. You may even decide to get the cards out amongst your friends so that they can join in the fun!

If you only memorize the first five cards you have easily enough information to give someone a short palm reading. How many cards you learn and how fast you go is entirely up to you. By learning all ten you will be able to give some-one a quite satisfying reading.

Please try and learn these cards in the order they are numbered. Learning the cards in order is a memory booster in itself.

Unlike other books you may have read on Palmistry, this book is mainly about communication. I believe that many traditional books on Palmistry, while good for the serious student, are too full of theory and not enough practice. This book is practice heavy and aims to teach you to say a lot about very little. It focuses on talking the talk. Without a voice, all the theory in the world won't turn you into an interesting, entertaining and communicative palm reader.

There is a practice section at the end of each card's description. The first part of these practice sections involves creating your own readings based on the actual definitions of an imaginary client's hand traits i.e.

Creative / Down To Earth

The second parts are based on the physical traits of the hand i.e.

Flat hand with gap 3rd & 4th

If you can't speak freely about the definitions, you won't have anything to say even if you do know what the hand markings mean! Doing these practice sections is vitally important. Reading palms is a practical pursuit. If you want to learn lots of interesting things about Palmistry for your own amusement but have little interest in actually giving readings then this is not the book for you. You will need to learn the information on each card, practice the exercises and read and re-read this book for it all to sink in. You can't learn unless you try, and this book is all about trying.

Use the cards. Do the exercises. Love the sound of your own voice. Speak up!

INTRODUCTION

There is the study of Palmistry, and then there is Palm Reading. One is theoretic, and the other is practical. It is no accident that this book is called 'Speed Learning ~ Palm Reading In Your Own Words' as it deals entirely with the act of giving people readings. As such, I feel it important to say a little about what people are expecting, what you should give them, and how you should make them feel.

Many people know a little about Palmistry. They probably know that there's a heart and a head line, and may know about the life line and its connection with longevity. They will also expect to find out something about their future. What is for certain is that once the word is out that you can 'read palms' you will have no shortage of people thrusting their hands in your face asking you to tell them their fortune.

With this in mind I usually say that, although I can tell quite a bit about someone by looking at their hands their fortune may be a bit more difficult, but by finding out what makes them tick I may be able to help them plan a better future. This helps distance me from 'fortune telling' and makes me appear a little more scientific, which for many people is a comfort. Also, it is a nice way to ask them to 'open up'. I have in effect told them that if they communicate with me I can help them, so it is in their best interests to cooperate.

I am helping them to help themselves. I am not making predictions.

Communication is a two way street, so one of the best things you can do when giving a palm reading is to leave lots of pauses to get some kind of response from the person whose hand you are studying. Sometimes you can have entire conversations between each hand comment! Let people talk about themselves, join in the conversation, and then connect what they are telling you with what you see in their hand.

When you first start reading someone's palm however, they are likely to be rather quiet as you start the reading. This is normal. Often you need to prompt them to join in the reading by asking them how you are doing. 'Does that make sense to you?' or something similar between each of your own comments, especially at the start of a palm reading lets the person know that they are expected to join in. Once you have got them used to nodding, agreeing or talking about each thing you say they will do it of their own accord. If you do not prompt them at the start however, you could find that you can get to the end of a palm reading without them having said a word. I would consider that a bad reading.

If you feel like you are having a conversation with someone about what they're like, based on what you see in their hand, then you are giving a good palm reading. If you feel like you've made a new friend after each and every palm reading, you are most definitely on the right track.

Don't just talk to the hand! Talk to the person. You're not looking at an antique, you're studying someone's palm - talk to the person it belongs to, and not to their hand! Take time to look up and engage in conversation, the hand will still be there when you look down again. This will help pace your reading and make it feel less like 'reading by numbers'.

Most people have never had their palm read properly, so they will probably be excited that someone who knows what they're talking about is going to read their palm. Don't disappoint them! Before you read each palm remember that there is a person attached to the other end who wants to feel like they have the most interesting palm you have ever set eyes upon. So if you see anything unusual in anyones hand, point it out! Not only that, no matter what is going on around you, make them the sole focus of your attention.

Being rejected by a palm reader is tantamount to being told you're not interesting, so if you really don't want to read any palms, simply say something like 'You look like a very interesting person and I'm sure your palm is fascinating, but I'm a little tired now and don't feel I could do you justice.' This is much better than a dismissive glance. The reason I know this is because reading several palms in one go can leave you rather drained and needing a break, and I found myself upsetting people by looking uninterested and tired out when approached about a reading, instead of courteous and polite. Be nice, and remember how excited the disappointed will be when you read their palms at a later time or date.

Be positive, upbeat and lighthearted. Make them feel good to be them, despite their foibles and traits. Big up the good traits, which always overcome the bad traits. Make them feel interesting, funny and unique.

Give them hope. It's what they, and you, deserve!

Julian Moore

CARD 1 : FIRST IMPRESSIONS 1

One of the first ways we can get an understanding of what the client is like is by the very way they show us their hand. This gesture can tell us a lot about them - do they thrust their hand in your face, or hold their hand out sheepishly?

Although this isn't 'reading their palm' so to speak, it is a good indicator of their general character, and will help you decipher their hand in a way relevant to them. When someone comes to you to have their palm read you shouldn't treat their hand as if it were disembodied in a vacuum! The hand is part of the body, and you really should take in the whole person into consideration before you start on the hand itself.

From this we can therefore make some other quick generalizations:

1a. HOW IS THE HAND PRESENTED TO YOU?

★If it's cupped then the person is probably quite shy and withdrawn and could be quite worried about what their hand will reveal about them
★If the hand is held out flat then the person is probably a fairly positive and outgoing type who is not particularly worried about what people think about them
★If the hand is extended as far out as it will go, then you are probably dealing with an extroverted and possibly overbearing individual!

Of course, the hand will most likely be shown to you somewhere between these examples, but always notice this initial contact with the client and bear it in mind when looking at the hand in general.

1b. WHICH FINGERS SHOW THE LARGEST GAPS?

★1st & 2nd Fingers = Confident / Good self esteem
★2nd & 3rd Fingers = Lives for the moment
★3rd & 4th Fingers = Independent thinker

The gaps can give you slightly more to go on, and when combined with the closeness of the thumb to the hand (shown on Card 4) can be another good indicator of temperament.

Even though this is the first card and there doesn't seem to be much information on it, do not underestimate the importance of using this simple information to get an overview of the client. By having a broad snapshot of the demeanor of the client you will understand their hand more *as it relates to them*.

For example, if the client shows you his hand in rather a shy way, but has rather a large thumb (showing MOTIVATION : Card 4) then you know he is quiet AND motivated. That's a lot of information already, but you need to relate that to him in a useful way. You could say something like 'You're quiet and reserved but have a silent motivation that gets things done.' This is a meaningful sentence that the client can relate to more than 'Your gaps show this and your thumb shows that.'

A key principle often overlooked by many of the palmistry books is that to make a reading actually mean something to the client you have to make a number of comparisons about the hand, and turn those into useful sentences.

You need to make sense and not just reel off a list of hand traits.

Another example, if the client shows you his outstretched hand (showing an extroverted nature) but you notice he has a tented arch (showing LACK OF CONFIDENCE : Card 5) then you could say something like 'You have learnt to overcome your lack of confidence by developing a larger than life personality'. Again, this makes much more sense than just saying 'You are an extrovert that lacks confidence'. Not only that it's less insulting!

By comparing only two traits you will ALWAYS have something useful to say even with the smallest amount of information.

If you combine that with the demeanor of the client you can say even more.

You may often find that the various meanings on the hand are contradictory, and while that may sound complicated it actually gives you a lot to go on. You need to practice explaining the contradictory traits more than the complimentary traits, but once you've practiced even a little you will realize that the contradictions in the hand can show you a lot about the client's innermost conflicts.

Basically, the traits that compliment each other are the ones most likely to be seen in the person day to day, and the contradictory traits show more of the 'inner struggle' of the client.

Practice 1

Here are some traits paired in groups. Create a meaningful mini-reading from each pair by combining their meanings and say them OUT LOUD: *

1. Shy / Lives for the moment
2. Positive / Confident
3. Positive / Independent thinker
4. Shy / Independent thinker
5. Extrovert / Lives for the moment
6. Extrovert / Confident

7. Cupped hand with gap 2nd & 3rd
8. Flat hand with gap 3rd & 4th
9. Extended hand with gap 1st & 2nd
10. Cupped hand with no gap

* There are some 'answers' to these questions in the back of the book

CARD 2: HAND SHAPE

Hand shape can tell you some immediate things about the client, based on the shape of the palm and the length of the fingers. More often than not, someone with long fingers has a long hand overall, and people with short fingers tend to have quite square palms. However, this is not always the case.

2a. WHAT SHAPE IS THE PALM?

★Square Palm = Practical
★Oblong Palm = Creative

When you first try and assess this trait you may find it quite tricky, but even after having looked at only a few hands it gets much easier. I tend to see if I can make out an oblong first, from the bottoms of the fingers down to the wrist. For some reason I find it easier to work out if the palm *ISN'T* an oblong than to see if it *IS* a square.

Memory tip: I've always remembered these traits by thinking that a practical kind of person would build a SQUARE house with just four simple square windows, but if they were more creative they'd make it tall and OB-LONG, with three or four levels and long windows.

2b. HOW LONG ARE THE FINGERS?

★Short Fingers = Quick Witted Doer
★Long Fingers = Time Taking Thinker

This is a bit easier to assess initially as you have the length of the hand to compare the fingers to. It's all about proportion really. With these four character traits we now have four types of hand:

HAND SHAPES

	Short fingers (quick witted doer)	Long fingers (time taking thinker)
Square palm (*Practical*)	Practical, quick witted doer	Practical, time taking thinker
Oblong palm (*Creative*)	Creative, quick witted doer	Creative, time taking thinker

Practice 2

As you now have two cards worth of information to play with you can now start mixing up the hand traits to arrive at some useful conclusions. See if you can give a mini-reading OUT LOUD in your OWN WORDS to an imagined client based on these sets of traits:

1. Shy / Lives for the moment / Creative, time taking thinker
2. Outgoing / Independent thinker / Practical, quick witted doer
3. Extroverted / Confident / Creative, quick witted doer
4. Outgoing / Lives for the moment / Practical, time taking thinker

What Do You Mean? The ever expanding question...

Don't forget, if you can't create a useful sentence or two from the actual descriptions of the traits, then you're not going to be much good when you see the traits on the hand. Always practice speaking out loud to an imaginary client! Even if you find you can't say much to start with, start anyway! You'll only get better at it!

One way of getting yourself started is to imagine a client who asks you 'What do you mean?' after everything you say. So for instance you say 'You are shy, you live for the moment, and you are a creative, time taking thinker' (which are just the stock definitions) and the imaginary client asks 'What do you mean?' so you then must try to expand it to something like 'You get a kick from doing things on the spur of the moment, apart from when you're being creative, when you like to take time to get things right. Although you have a spontaneous streak, you tend to keep yourself to yourself and only let it out when the time suits you.', and then the imaginary client asks 'What do you mean?' and you continue....

By practicing this ever expanding explanation from the simple to the complex you will gain invaluable practice in getting your mouth in gear, which is actually far harder than learning the meanings of the hand traits! It is one thing to learn what the traits of the hand actually mean, and quite another to actually communicate that to someone smoothly and effectively.

3. FIRST IMPRESSIONS 2 – 'CUFFS'

Card number three is mainly to do with how the hand actually feels to the touch. By judging the colour, feel, flexibility and sponginess of the hand you can tell an awful lot about someone.

To remember which things you should be checking for you can use the acronym '**CUFFS**' as follows:

CU	F	F	S
Colour	**Feel**	**Flexibility**	**Sponginess**

As someone's shirt cuffs will more often than not be staring you in the face when you're giving a reading, this memory booster is pretty easy to remember! Even if they're not, it's easy to remember that CUFFS are usually close to the hand covering the wrist.

3a. WHAT OVERALL COLOUR IS THE HAND? (CU)

The colour of the hand can be a general indicator of the clients current health. These are guidelines and must be taken into account with the rest of the traits on this card.

WHITE	YELLOW	BLUE	PINK	RED
Lack of energy	Jaundiced view	Bad circulation	Healthy	Energy

If their hand is white as a sheet then this probably shows a lack of energy, and particularly white and almost translucent skin can show fragility.

Yellow signifies someone who has a jaundiced view of the world. However, you should be careful not to confuse this with Orientals or heavy smokers!

15

A blue hand can often indicate bad circulation, but age can play a large part in a hand's apparent blueness.

Pink hands are usually healthy, and red hands show energy and vitality. The only time this doesn't hold true is when the client is of a ruddy disposition and the redness in the hands show exertion due to a less than perfect lifestyle.

3b. HOW DOES THE SKIN FEEL? (F)

The overall feel of the hand must be taken into consideration along with the hand colour.

   ★Fine = Refined
   ★Course = Down to earth

There are parallels with the feel and colour of the hand with the hand shape it-self. Quite often, people with square palms (Practical) also have normal to course hand texture. People with oblong palms (Creative) very often have smooth fine hands.
It's a simple task to judge the feel of the hand as you are holding it! Just be-cause a hand has many lines does not mean that it still can't be smooth to the touch.

It's not rocket science to deduce whether someone is more likely to be a pianist or a builder from the feel of their hands, so use your common sense too.

3c. HOW FLEXIBLE ARE THE FINGERS? (F)

To tell how flexible a persons hand is, you need to push back their fingers and see how far the thumb pushes back. Some people's fingers go way back at right angles to the hand, and some hardly budge.

   ★Flexible = Adaptable
   ★Rigid = Flexible / Stubborn

When judging this trait you also need to take into account the clients age. For instance, a person whose hand is still flexible in old age shows that as they've grown older, they've still remained open to new ideas and challenges. A younger person with a rigid hand is probably someone who has become set in their ways quite early on in life and may face challenges in the future when their way of seeing things doesn't always work.

3d. HOW SPONGY OR HARD IS THE PALM? (S)

Sponginess isn't about smoothness, it's about bounce and fleshiness. Is someone's hand firm to the touch, or even hard, or is is fleshy and bouncy? Some peoples hands are very hard and flat, and others are soft and squishy. It's easy to tell by simply squeezing different parts of the palm.

★Spongy = Sensual pleasure seeking
★Hard = Practical hard working

People with fleshier hands tend to be bigger and bouncier people anyway, and people with hard flat hands tend to be more on the athletic side.
The four indicators of colour, feel, flexibility and sponginess should all be assessed at the same time. The make up of the hand tends to be fairly uniform, and it is seldom that you find someone with conflicting sets of traits from these particular indicators.

Practice 3

Using just the traits from Card 3, see if you can give a mini-reading OUT LOUD in your OWN WORDS to an imagined client based on these sets:

1. Lack of energy / Refined / Inflexible / Sensual pleasure seeking
2. Healthy / Down to earth / Adaptable / Practical hard working
3. Energy / Refined / Inflexible / Sensual pleasure seeking
4. Jaundiced view / Down to earth / Adaptable / Practical hard working

5. White / Course / Flexible / Hard
6. Blue / Fine / Rigid / Spongy
7. Red / Course / Rigid / Hard
8. Pink / Fine / Flexible / Spongy

CONTRADICTIONS ARE GOOD FOR YOU

As you try to create useful readings from these practice tests, you may find that even though you thought that having sets of traits which were complimentary were much easier to talk about, quite the opposite is true.

These traits:

Healthy / Down to earth / Adaptable / Practical hard working

are so complimentary they almost cancel themselves out! They all point to the same thing, and don't really tell you much about the person that you couldn't have easily found out about already. You will find that although it's good to find the commonalities in a persons hand, it's the *differences* which yield the most interesting information.
The set of traits above show someone who's a nice, hard working but easy going kind of guy. When you simply change one of the traits thus:

Healthy / Down to earth / **Inflexible** / Practical hard working

you have a lot more to go on as you now have something that could be perceived as *negative* in the mix. This set of traits shows someone who's a hard working kind of guy who needs to avoid being set in his ways and see the bigger picture. There is something more interesting to say simply because *Adaptable* was changed to *Inflexible*.

It's very nice when someone's hand shows a lot of similar traits as it defines them more quickly, but it doesn't really help you give them any advice. As a reader you are not only telling people what they are like, but what to watch out for - some of the pitfalls in their personality which could hinder their progress and they should be made aware of. Without differences and conflicts you will have very little to tell someone, so you need to bring up the differences at every opportunity. That is why is it good to scan the hand and find at least two conflicting traits each time you want to speak.

19

You can start by describing an undesirable trait and then back it up with a good one:

> 'Although you have trouble keeping your energy levels up (noticing their white hands), you are able to compensate for this with your resilient nature (noticing their larger than average thumb)'

or you could do it the other way around:

> 'You are able to switch from one task to another effortlessly (noticing their flexible fingers) but are easily distracted from the matter in hand when something more appealing shows up (noticing sensual pleasure seeking)'

Switching between these two modes of communication is extremely effective and keeps the reading flowing.

CARDS 1–3 RECAP

Even though we've only looked at three cards, you are in a good position to be able to tell someone quite a lot about themselves just by looking at their hand.

- The way the hand is presented to you can tell something about the client's personality. By the spaces between their fingers you can tell even more.

- By looking at the shape of the palm and the lengths of the fingers you can see how they approach life.

- By judging the hand's colour, feel, flexibility and sponginess (CUFFS) you can see how healthy, refined, adaptable and practical they are.

REVISION 1

We're now going to mix the information on these three cards together.

See if you can give a short mini-reading about each one of these hands

HAND 1	Presentation	Gaps	Hand shape	Finger length
	Cupped	3rd & 4th	Oblong	Long
	CU: White / **F:** Refined / **F:** Flexible / **S:** Hard			

HAND 2	Presentation	Gaps	Hand shape	Finger length
	Extended	1st & 2nd	Square	Long
	CU: Red / **F:** Course / **F:** Inflexible / **S:** Soft			

HAND 3	Presentation	Gaps	Hand shape	Finger length
	Flat	2nd & 3rd	Square	Short
	CU: Yellow / **F:** Course / **F:** Flexible / **S:** Soft			

(Use the cards for reference if you have to, and if it helps, try typing out your answers and spending a bit of time on them)

21

CARD 4: THE THUMB

4a. HOW BIG IS THE THUMB?

★Large = Motivated
★Small = Easygoing

People with big thumbs tend to be more motivated than those with smaller thumbs. Smaller thumbs indicate a less forceful personality, and very small thumbs on a larger hand can show a severe lack of drive and confidence.

> **Memory tip:** I always imagine someone with a large thumb not being afraid to stick it out to 'thumb a lift' through life, and people with small thumbs perhaps aren't too bothered about hitching a ride and don't mind walking some of the distance. People with very small thumbs are almost too afraid of hitchhiking to even stick their thumb out so will probably not bother.

4b. WHICH THUMB PHALANGE IS BIGGEST?

★Top phalange = Willpower
★Bottom phalange = Logic

You need to assess the difference in size between the last two phalanges of the thumb. This can be done by holding the top of the thumb against the side of the middle phalange of the other hand's thumb.

This tells you whether the client uses Willpower or Logic to overcome his obstacles in life. Sometimes there is a balance between the two and occasionally there is a big difference.

> **Memory tip:** I always remember that the end phalange of the thumb is WILLPOWER because if I want to push a drawing pin into a board I have to FORCE it in with the end of my thumb.

4c. HOW CLOSE IS THE THUMB TO THE HAND?

★Close to the hand = Shrewd
★Away from hand = Outgoing / Generous

This is similar to seeing how extended someone's hand is except the thumb is a little more revealing.

Practice 4

Using just the traits from Card 4, see if you can give a short mini-reading OUT LOUD in your OWN WORDS to an imagined client based on these sets:

1. Motivated / Logic / Shrewd
2. Easygoing / Willpower / Generous
3. Motivated / Willpower / Shrewd
4. Easygoing / Logic / Generous

5. Small thumb / Larger top phalange / Close to hand
6. Large thumb / Larger bottom phalange / Away from hand
7. Large thumb / Larger top phalange / Away from hand
8. Small thumb / Larger bottom phalange / Close to hand

CARD 5: FINGER SETTINGS

The finger settings are judged by drawing an imaginary line across the bottom of the fingers where they meet the palm. This line tends to create either a straight line, a curved arch, a tented arch or shows that the little finger is quite a bit lower than the other fingers.

HOW ARE THE FINGERS SET ON THE HAND?

★Straight Line = Confident and proud
★Curved Arch = Well balanced / Fair / Easygoing
★Tented Arch = Lacking confidence / Low self - esteem
★Dropped Little Finger = Life struggle

Memory tip: You can imagine a straight line representing a confident and proud person quite easily, and the curved line representing someone more flexible, easygoing and less rigid. Also, if you imagine that same confidence being snapped in the middle to represent low self-esteem, and the line being totally off-center at one end to represent life struggle, you will easily re-member these traits.

Again we are starting to see some similarities between these traits and some of the ones that have gone before, but now you have more to play with, the chances that some of these will conflict with previous traits will be as I've said before, useful.

Practice 5

Using the traits from cards 4 & 5, see if you can give a mini-reading OUT LOUD in your OWN WORDS to an imagined client based on these sets:

1. Motivated / Logic / Shrewd : Confident and proud
2. Easygoing / Willpower / Generous : Life struggle
3. Motivated / Willpower / Shrewd : Easygoing
4. Easygoing / Logic / Generous : Low self - esteem

5. Large thumb / Larger bottom phalange / Away from hand
   Dropped little finger
6. Large thumb / Larger top phalange / Away from hand
   Fingers set in a straight line
7. Small thumb / Larger bottom phalange / Close to hand
   Fingers set in a tented arch

Using just the traits from cards 3, 4 and 5, see if you can give a mini-reading OUT LOUD in your OWN WORDS to an imagined client based on these sets:

8. Lack of energy / Refined / Inflexible / Sensual pleasure seeking
   Motivated / Willpower/ Shrewd
   Life struggle
9. Healthy / Down to earth / Adaptable / Practical hard working
   Easygoing / Logic / Generous
   Confident and proud

10. Blue / Fine / Rigid / Spongy
    Large thumb / Larger top phalange / Away from hand
    Fingers set in a curved arch
11. Red / Course / Rigid / Hard
    Small thumb / Smaller top phalange / Close to hand
    Fingers set in a straight line

CARDS 1–5 RECAP

Now we've got five cards to play with let's have a look at all the information available to us in one go:

- The way the hand is presented to you can tell something about the client's personality. By the spaces between their fingers you can tell even more.

- By looking at the shape of the palm and the lengths of the fingers you can see how they approach life.

- By judging the hand's colour, feel, flexibility and sponginess (CUFFS) you can see how healthy, refined, adaptable and practical they are.

- By looking at the thumb we can see how motivated and outgoing they are, and whether they use willpower or logic to succeed.

- The settings of the fingers tell us how confident they are and how they feel about themselves.

REVISION 2

See if you can match each trait up with it's description:

Short fingers	Extroverted	Energy	Square hand	Inflexible	Jaundiced view
Inflexible fingers	Bad circulation	Gap between 2 & 3	Practical hard working	Confident	Fine hand
White hand	Positive	Sensual pleasure seeking	Pink hand	Course hand	Oblong hand
Motivated	Small thumb	Quick witted doer	Cupped hand	Large thumb	Flexible fingers
Refined	1st thumb phalange long	Shrewd	Healthy	Independent thinker	Spongy palm
Red hand	Creative	Logic	Lack of energy	Blue hand	Gap between 1 & 2
Extended hand	Thumb held away from hand	Practical	Outgoing	2nd thumb phalange long	Down to earth
Adaptable	Easy going	Shy	Thumb held close to hand	Gap between 3 & 4	Long fingers
Time taking thinker	Yellow hand	Willpower	Lives for the moment	Hard palm	Flat hand
Confident	Lower little finger	Curved set fingers	Life struggle	Straight set fingers	Well balanced

In this grid, one pair of description/trait is missing? Which is it?

27

REVISION 2 : FIVE CARD RECAP ~ descriptions

Shy	Positive	Extroverted
Confident	Lives for the moment	Independent thinker

Practical	Creative
Quick witted doer	Time taking thinker

Lack of energy	Jaundiced view	Bad circulation	Healthy	Energy

Refined	Down to earth
Adaptable	Inflexible
Sensual pleasure seeking	Practical hard working

Motivated	Easy going
Willpower	Logic
Shrewd	Outgoing

Confident	Well balanced	Lacking confidence	Life struggle

Without looking at the opposite page (unless you get stuck):
Try to remember which trait each description goes with
Give a mini-reading OUT LOUD in your OWN WORDS by going down the
list and picking a random description from each line

REVISION 2 : FIVE CARD RECAP ~ traits

Cupped hand	Flat hand	Extended hand
Gap between 1 & 2	Gap between 2 & 3	Gap between 3 & 4

Square hand	Oblong hand
Short fingers	Long fingers

White hand	Yellow hand	Blue hand	Pink hand	Red hand

Fine hand	Course hand
Flexible fingers	Inflexible fingers
Spongy palm	Hard palm

Large thumb	Small thumb
1st thumb phalange longer than 2nd	2nd thumb phalange longer than 1st
Thumb held close to hand	Thumb held away from hand

Straight set fingers	Curved set fingers	Tented arch	Lower little finger

Without looking at the opposite page (unless you get stuck):
Try to remember which description each trait goes with
Give a mini-reading OUT LOUD in your OWN WORDS by going down the
list and picking a random trait from each line

A BRIEF INTERLUDE

We've seen how the various hand traits can be combined to provide meaningful insights for the client so that they can relate to what you are saying. Reading someone's palm is about communication, and although there is a science to what the different hand shapes and lines actually mean, this is lost without the means to deliver this information with any relevance.

We are dealing with human beings, and most people who have their palm read want to know about 'The Future'. What would you like to know about the future if YOU went for a palm reading? You would probably like to know if your career was going to go the way you wanted, if your relationship was going to stay on the right track or even if you were going to meet that special someone.

You know what people want the answers to, as they have the same questions as you do. But how does this relate to palm reading?

Well, at this stage and only five cards into this book you should now be able to see a few commonalities and differences in a person's hand, and be able to come up with a reasonable profile for them. As we've discussed, by looking at the commonalities we can find out a persons type and their common strengths, and by looking at the differences and contradictions we can find the things that they must watch out for in order to succeed in life.

You can apply this information to almost any type of question. Imagine you have a friend who you know is a bit over the top and has a very forceful nature. If he asked you to tell him what he should do about his love life, you would probably tell him that although he likes to be the center of attention, this can sometimes work against him and make it hard for people to get to know him.

If you had a friend who was quite a nervous and shy character and he asked you about the new business he had started, you would probably tell him that he should make sure that he sells the idea enough and not to hide in the office, and if he is not a natural salesman, to hire someone who is!

What I'm saying here is, you already KNOW the answers to all these questions, it's the kind of advice we give our friends and family daily, and are the very questions we ourselves ask of others.

So how does this apply to a palm reading? Unless someone has specifically come for a palmistry one-on-one session (which is way beyond the scope of this book), then more often than not, they just want their palm read and have no particular question in mind. But what we DO know is that just like everyone else in the world, their main concerns will be money, career, love and health. We can apply that to what we see in their hand.

As I've said before, your main aim is to be RELEVANT to the client. By applying what you see in their hand to the very things that most people want to know about, you will be very relevant indeed.

Imagine that you have a friend who is very creative, but sometimes finds it hard to see things through. He can be quite defensive at times, and finds it hard when he doesn't get his own way. What would YOU tell him about his approach to money, career, and love life?

You could say something like 'You have a highly creative streak which opens a lot of doors for you, however if you truly want to make money with your current endeavors you must keep an eye on the accounts, even though you'd rather be coming up with new and interesting schemes. You need to learn that to progress with your current affairs you're going to need to to cooperate with people you don't necessarily agree with, but taking things less personally you will be able to spend more time doing what you do best and spend less time worrying. This applies to your love life too, as when you're in a relationship you can get a bit picky and find it hard to admit you're wrong. In the past this has caused a few upsets, but as you grow older you will learn that you're only human and that your loved ones only have your best interests at heart.'

As you can see, by applying this friend's character type to money, career and love life we were able to give him quite a lot of information. If we had also included health, we could have told him how healthy an individual he was from his hand colour and general demeanor, and by judging his character, tell him

31

how to improve his overall health, and if he was unhealthy, explain the mental blocks that could have been hindering his progress.

While you're giving a palm reading, the client may well relax after a while and ask you specific questions. By practicing giving readings based on the four most commonly asked questions it should be no trouble to give some advice based on a specific question.

Another thing that should be pointed out is that if there is a predominance of a particular trait in the hand, then there could be too much of a good thing! Someone with a hand whose traits point predominantly to being strong and forceful could be an overpowering bully! Someone with too much creativity could be a dreamer. When you judge the hand look for BALANCE, and judge things accordingly.

CARD 6: FINGER MEANINGS (ARCC)

The fingers all have names and represent a particular trait:

(Thumb)	Name	Meaning	Other Meanings
1st Finger	**J**upiter	**A**mbition	Independence Confidence
2nd Finger	**S**aturn	**R**esponsibility	Limitations Common Sense
3rd Finger	**A**pollo	**C**reativity	Self Expression Aesthetic Sense
4th Finger	**M**ercury	**C**ommunication	Business Quick Thinking

It's useful to know the names of the fingers as it's easier to refer to them by a name and not a number. Also, when you're giving a reading it's interesting for the client to hear you use the names Jupiter, Saturn, Apollo and Mercury.

Memory tip: To remember the names of the fingers you have the letters JSAM. I have always remembered this by the magical expression 'Shazam!' (J-sam!)

To remember the traits of each finger it is easy to remember the word ARC. It's almost 'ABC', and the R in the middle looks very like a B.

Even though there are two C's at the end, I remember that the Mercury finger is communication by holding an 'imaginary telephone' to my head where the little finger is the mouthpiece (communication).

The first thing you are looking at is relative finger length. Taking the length of all the fingers into consideration, is one of the fingers noticeably longer than average for that type of finger? Or is one of the fingers shorter for that type of finger?

If the length isn't giving you any clues, look at the thickness of the fingers. Is one finger thicker or thinner than another?

As you can guess by now, the longer or bigger a finger is, the more it's traits have dominance. Someone with a longer/bigger than average Saturn finger is a responsible type and gets though life by using common sense. Conversely, someone with a noticeably small Saturn finger can tend to be irresponsible and rash.

Another very important thing to look out for is for the curve and bend in peoples fingers. A bend in the finger weakens it, and if one finger is leaning towards another, it is leaning on that finger's trait to compensate for its own weakness. This is not necessarily a bad thing and simply shows which traits the client has leant on through life.

The fleshy pads on the palm at the base of each finger are called the Mounts of Jupiter, Saturn, Apollo and Mercury respectively. These pads show how much stored up energy each of the corresponding fingers has. This is energy that has yet to be used, and can indicate resources that the client is for some reason or another unable to tap into at the present time. An actual hollow at the base of one of the fingers can mean that all the available resources for that finger have been used up.

Here's an analogy. Imagine that the fingers are four palm trees in a line. The strongest tree stands completely straight, and the other trees bend towards it for protection. The unhealthy looking trees either have no water reserves left, or have had their reserves cut off. The healthy trees are able to access their water supply with no problem. Some of the unhealthy trees will have to wait for rain, the others will have to grow roots to reach their reserves.

By using this analogy we can see that some finger traits are dominant, and the other traits lean in that direction to make up for their own weakness. Some traits are frustrated as they do not have sufficient energy to be used, and will either have to simply wait for the energy to return OR find a way to tap the energy that is currently dormant. A strong finger with a healthy but not overly raised mount is drawing its strength from the well evenly and it's traits are in full effect. As always, it's a question of balance.

For example, a strong Apollo finger with a dipped mount can show severe creative frustration - even though the finger has great potential it must lie dormant until the time is right. The creative inspiration will have to wait. The same finger with a raised mount is also frustrating, but shows untapped sources of energy. By looking in other places for inspiration and with a bit of lateral thinking, inspiration can be found if the client is willing to look for it.

By using the length, size and bend in the fingers, along with the Mounts of each finger, we can build up quite a detailed picture of the client's path through life and his hidden potential. This is the point where we can really expand on what has gone before.

Cupping the hand can help tell how fleshy the Mounts are when you're unsure.

<u>Practice 6</u>

Using just the traits from Card 6, see if you can give a mini-reading OUT LOUD in your OWN WORDS to an imagined client based on these sets. The plus signs show an abundance of a trait and the minus signs show that the trait is lacking. The letter 'N' shows that the trait is 'normal'.

1. + Ambition / N Responsibility / N Creativity / N Communication
2. N Ambition / - Responsibility / - Creativity / N Communication
3. N Ambition / N Responsibility / N Creativity / + Communication
4. + Ambition / + Responsibility / N Creativity / N Communication

In the next set, the less than and more than signs (< and >) are used to show if a trait is *leaning* towards another:

5. - Ambition < N Responsibility / + Creativity / N Communication
6. N Ambition / N Responsibility > N Creativity > - Communication
7. N Ambition > N Responsibility / - Creativity / + Communication
8. + Ambition / N Responsibility / N Creativity < N Communication

Here are some sets using the 'real' names of the fingers:

9. N Jupiter > N Saturn / - Apollo < N Mercury
10. - Jupiter / - Saturn < N Apollo > - Mercury
11. + Jupiter / N Saturn > - Apollo > + Mercury
12. N Jupiter < N Saturn < N Apollo / + Mercury

Here are some sets using the numbers of the fingers:

13. N 1st / N 2nd / - 3rd < N 4th
14. - 1st > - 2nd > N 3rd > - 4th
15. + 1st < N 2nd < - 3rd > + 4th
16. N 1st / N 2nd < N 3rd / + 4th

If you're finding all this a little confusing, first look to see which fingers are the most dominant and which are the weakest and talk about that. Then reflect on THAT information by looking at the way the fingers are leaning and discuss how the leaning effects the dominant and weak fingers.

THE LINES OF THE HAND

Most people when they think of Palmistry think of the lines, and even people with a passing interest often know that there is a Heart Line, a Life Line and a Head Line.

★The Heart Line is the top line nearest the fingers, and represents the emotions.

★The Head Line is the middle line and represents our thoughts.

★The Life Line is the bottom line that curves around the thumb, and represents life energy.

By comparing the size, length, start and end points of the lines on the hand we have yet more clues to the inner workings of the client.

CARD 7: HEART LINE

The heart line is the 'top' line of the hand. It deals with the emotions.

7a. STRAIGHT ACROSS OR BENDS TOWARDS FINGERS?

★Straight Across = Sensitive and needy
★Bends Towards Fingers = Open hearted / Expressive

> **Memory Tip:** We use our fingers to reach out and touch the world around us. If the Heart Line curves up towards the fingers this shows the ability to be open with emotions and express that out into the world. A Heart Line that goes straight across the hand is the opposite - it shows that the world is expected to fulfill the emotional needs of the individual and the fingers seek to draw that in.

7b. WHERE DOES IT END?

★Beneath 1st finger (Jupiter) = Emotionally open / Romantically idealistic
★Beneath 2nd finger (Saturn) = Emotionally closed / Loner
★Between 1st and 2nd finger = Emotionally balanced

By seeing where the Heart Line ends we are basically judging the length of the line in proportion to the hand. A long Heart Line shows an emotionally open individual, a short Heart Line shows an emotionally closed loner.

Again there may be contradictions in this line. A Heart Line which bends towards the fingers (open hearted and expressive) but is rather short (emotionally closed) may show someone who is all open arms when they first meet someone, but as soon as they get too close they simply shut down emotionally. Use contradictions to your advantage, especially between the three major lines themselves.

<u>Practice 7</u>

Using just the traits from Card 7, see if you can say OUT LOUD in your OWN WORDS something useful to an imagined client based on these sets:

1. Sensitive and needy / Emotionally closed
2. Open hearted / Emotionally closed
3. Sensitive and needy / Emotionally balanced
4. Open hearted / Emotionally open

5. Heart line bends towards fingers / Long
6. Heart line straight across palm / Short
7. Heart line bends towards fingers / Between
8. Heart line straight across palm / Long

CARD 8: HEAD LINE

The Head Line is the middle line of the hand and represents thought process.

8a. HOW LONG IS THE HEAD LINE?

★Long = Detailed thinker
★Short = Quick thinker

You'll notice that this is almost the same idea as the lengths of the fingers - the longer the Head Line, the more 'thinking' there is going on, the shorter it is the quicker the thought process.

8b. IS THE HEAD LINE STRAIGHT OR CURVED?

★Straight = Logical / Down to earth
★Curves to wrist = Creative

Again in a similar way to the Heart Line, the relationship of the Head Line with the fingers is important. If the Head Line runs straight across the palm keeping towards the finger side of the hand, the thought processes are drawn towards practicalities. If the Head Line curves away from the fingers somewhat towards the wrist, the thought process are reflected inwards to the more creative inner self.

8c. HOW CLOSE IS THE HEAD LINE TO THE LIFE LINE?

★Touches Life Line = Impulsive
★Away from life line = Cautious

The Life Line deals with our life energy. It stands to reason that if someone's Head Line is touching their Life Line then their thoughts and actions are hard-wired together and they can tend to act quite impulsively. If their Head Line is totally separate from their Life Line, then their thoughts would only result in action after some deliberation.

Practice 8

Using just the traits from Card 8, see if you can say OUT LOUD in your OWN WORDS something useful to an imagined client based on these sets:

1. Detailed thinker / Creative / Impulsive
2. Quick thinker / Logical / Cautious
3. Detailed thinker / Logical / Impulsive
4. Quick thinker / Creative / Cautious

5. Short Head Line / Straight / Touches Life Line
6. Long Head Line / Curves to wrist / Away from Life Line
7. Short Head Line / Straight / Away from Life Line
8. Long Head Line / Curves to wrist / Touches Life Line

CARD 9: LIFE LINE

9a. HOW WIDE DOES THE LIFE LINE SWEEP AROUND THE THUMB?

★Big sweep = Energy
★Close to thumb = Lacking energy

(I find it useful to give the size of the 'sweep' around the thumb a number from one to ten - this helps fix in your mind how much energy the person has based on other hands you have seen)

The Life Line sweeps around the base of the thumb so the more of an arc it takes around the base of the thumb, the longer it is. People with long Life Lines have a lot of vitality and energy whereas people with small life lines that hug the thumb can be quite lethargic.

9b. WHERE DOES THE LIFE LINE START?

★Near first finger = Ambitious
★Close to thumb = Humble
★Equal between first finger and thumb = Practical

As we know the first finger (Jupiter) is the finger of ambition and drive, so it is no surprise to find that the closer the Life Line starts up the hand towards the Jupiter finger, the more ambition the client has! Most life lines start halfway between the thumb joint and the fingers so it is quite easy to tell when someone has a Life Line that starts either closer or further away from the fingers.

By 'practical' in this instance we are dealing with ambition, so someone whose life line starts near the centre of the space between the first finger and thumb is someone who understands the practicalities of getting what they want.

<u>Practice 9</u>

Using just the traits from Card 9, see if you can say OUT LOUD in your OWN WORDS something useful to an imagined client based on these sets:

1. Energy / Ambition
2. Lacking energy / Humble
3. Energy / Humble
4. Lacking energy / Practical

5. Life Line sweeps around thumb / Starts close to the thumb
6. Life Line hugs thumb / Starts close to the first finger
7. Life Line sweeps around thumb / Starts close to the first finger
8. Life Line hugs thumb / Starts close to the thumb

CARDS 7-9 RECAP (MAJOR LINES)

By looking at the following tables one at a time (unless you get stuck):
Try to remember which description each trait goes with and vice-versa
Give a mini-reading OUT LOUD in your OWN WORDS by going down either
list and picking a random trait from each line

REVISION THREE: MAJOR LINES RECAP ~ descriptions

Sensitive & needy	Open hearted & expressive	
Emotionally open	Emotionally closed	
Detailed thinker	Quick thinker	
Logical	Creative	
Cautious	Impulsive	
Energy	Lacking energy	
Ambitious	Humble	Practical

REVISION THREE: MAJOR LINES RECAP ~ traits

Heart: Straight across	Heart: Bends towards fingers	
Heart: Ends under 1st finger	Heart: Ends under 2nd finger	
Head: Long	Head: Short	
Head: Straight	Head: Curves to wrist	
Head: Touches life line	Head: Away from life line	
Life: Big sweep around thumb	Life: Hugs thumb	
Life: Starts near first finger	Life: Starts close to thumb	Life: Starts inbetween

44

CARD 10: THE MINOR LINES

These are the most commonly found minor lines on the hand, and can add a little bit more spice to a reading when they are present. If you are unsure about a line, don't be afraid to slightly cup the hand of the client to see where the line could be.

On the cards, the lettering for each trait goes around the hand in two circles, A to D and E to H. Try to learn one 'revolution' at a time to stop you getting confused!

ARE THESE LINES PRESENT?

A: The **Intuition Line** curves up onto the palm from the side opposite the thumb. Having an intuition line shows someone who is able to rely on their hunches and feelings a great deal, but may not be fully aware of this talent. The longer the line is, the more intuitive they may be, with a very long line representing possible psychic ability.

B: The **Relationship Lines** can be found coming onto the hand from the sides just below the little finger. These show the potential for close relationships some which may not have been fulfilled. As these lines are below the Mercury finger (Communication) it's easy to remember that they are to do with other people. If you have difficulty seeing these lines then closing the hand a little can help define them. Laymen often mistake Relationship Lines for Children Lines.

C: The **Ring of Solomon** is the line that sometimes form under the 1st finger in an arc. Someone with this line has the power of the Jupiter finger but with the humanity and intuition to be strong but wise.

D: The **Family Chain** is found on all hands to some degree, so the thing to look at here is how 'chained' the line is. The deeper and more chains there are on this line, the more family orientated the person is.

45

E: The Via **Lasciva** crops up occasionally and shows a person who needs constant stimulation, which in itself can lead to all kind of problems. There is the possibility of an addictive personality, someone who 'doesn't know when to stop', and this can lead to strained personal relationships.

F: Children Lines shows how many children the client could potentially have. If the client already has children, it shows how many of them are emotionally close to him. Like the Relationship Lines, they are below the Mercury finger (Communication) which can help you remember that they are to do with other people.

G: People with the **Sympathy Line** have a sympathetic outlook on life, and spend a fair amount of time on other peoples concerns and can be overly empathic. If the line is strong, they may care more about others than themselves.

H: The Rascettes are also known as bracelets. Should the top ring curve up into the palm there may be difficulties giving birth. Imagining this curve as a bump can help you remember what it means!

FINAL WORD

Well if you've got this far you're either now a competent palm reader, or you're simply coming around for another revision! While you're here I'm just going to recap three important points:

1. Always try to find two traits which you can play off each other

2. Keep expanding on what you've said before - join up the traits

3. Take into account the things most people want to know about themselves

If you do these three things, you will be able to give someone a very satisfactory reading.

Here's some other things you can do to learn as quickly as possible:

1. Take the cards with you wherever you go so you can practice when you've got some spare time

2. When you're getting started, don't be afraid to use the cards as an aid to help you give a palm reading!

3. Don't just practice learning the markings - practice 'talking the talk' just as much, even when you're just beginning. *The sooner you do this the sooner you will be able to give meaningful readings.*

4. Look at as many hands as you can of your family and friends, not to give a reading, but just to have a look! You will be amazed how different everybody's hand is, and by simply looking you will get used to 'searching' for traits.

5. Don't forget, there is no such thing as failure. Anything you say about some-one's hand will be received with great excitement and is probably the most exciting thing that happened to them all week. Be warm and friendly and a little knowledge can go a long way!

I wish you every success with your new found skill. By following this book and using the cards, you can't fail to learn to read palms quickly, and to come across as sincere and interested. After all, it's all your own words!

Good luck!

Julian Moore

PRACTICE ANSWERS

(First ten questions only from Practice 1)

There are no right or wrong ways to structure your own readings, and the point of this whole book is to teach you how to find your own voice when it comes to giving palm readings. However, it can be quite daunting at first and hopefully these 'answers' will help get your brain and mouth functioning in unison! As this book is about finding your own voice, I recommend that you READ THESE ANSWERS OUT LOUD. That way you can truly get a 'feel' for what works for you and what doesn't.

Do not under any circumstances start LEARNING these answers as if they were the only truth. Use them to kick start your own thinking. Why not read my answers, and try and expand on them? Or read all the answers before going back to the questions and trying to say the same thing *in your own words*. After all, that's what this book is all about.

These are only the 'answers' for the first ten practices in the book and are here to help you get started. Once you get the idea, you'll easily be able to come up with your own words!

1. Shy / Lives for the moment

Although you can be shy at times you have a spontaneous streak which can sometimes take people by surprise.

2. Positive / Confident

You are an outgoing kind of person and you don't usually question your actions. People feel comfortable with you because of your open personality.

3. Positive / Independent thinker

You have an upbeat character but instead of simply joining in with the crowd you like to do things your own way. You are happy doing what pleases YOU, and this can be quite infectious as you always have fun doing it.

4. Shy / Independent thinker

You like to keep yourself to yourself and sometimes think that not everybody thinks like you do. You are quite happy to go your own way through life, although sometimes it can be a little lonely.

5. Extrovert / Lives for the moment

You are an extremely outgoing person who gets high on life. You like to be the center of attention and you're always up to something new, although your calmer friends think you should look before you leap.

6. Extrovert / Confident

You have a breezy approach to life and tend to sail through even the hardest times. Your optimistic nature and broad outlook make you friends wherever you go.

7. Cupped hand with gap 2nd & 3rd

Shy / Lives for the moment

I previously wrote:

Although you can be shy at times you have a spontaneous streak which can sometimes take people by surprise.

but how about:

You can get very excited about doing things on the spur of the moment, but sometimes your placid nature can hold you back.

8. Flat hand with gap 3rd & 4th

Positive / Independent thinker
I previously wrote:

You have an upbeat character but instead of simply joining in with the crowd you like to do things your own way. You are happy doing what pleases YOU, and this can be quite infectious as you always have fun doing it.

But what about:

You tend to think differently to other people and you have turned this to your advantage.

9. Extended hand with gap 1st & 2nd

Extrovert / Confident

I previously wrote:

You have a breezy approach to life and tend to sail through even the hardest times. Your optimistic nature and broad outlook make you friends wherever you go.

But what about:

You have a strong and resilient nature and can usually see the good in all situations. You tend to look outward and not inward and are not afraid of being yourself.

10. Cupped hand with no gap

Shy / Closed

(You are dealing with a VERY shy and nervous person here. So be nice!)

You tend to keep yourself to yourself and are a bit of a loner. This has been difficult sometimes but you've always pulled through. Sometimes you don't feel like 'all the others' but that's fine, as you probably know a lot more about what's going on than people would give you credit for.

Printing & Technical

Download / Flash Cards

This ebook comes with a PDF document containing the ten flash cards that you can use to learn the system.

You can download the flashcards when you register this book at:

http://thecoldreadingcompany.co.uk/coldreading/pflash

They have been designed to print onto index cards which measure 4 inches by 6 inches (10.16 cm X 15.24 cm).

The easiest way I have found to do this is:

First:

- Choose 4X6 in the print menu when choosing paper size
- Make sure the print preferences are set to 'landscape'

Then:

- Put 5 blank index cards in the printer short side in
- Print pages 1-10 with 'odd pages only' selected
- When those are printed, take them out together and place them back into the printer feeder blank side out ready for printing again
- Print pages 1-10 with 'even pages only' selected

And then:

- Repeat with another 5 blank cards for pages 11-20

Doing 5 cards at a time front and back is a lot easier than doing ten at a time!

Audiobook

You can download the audiobook that accompanies this text for free from:

http://thecoldreadingcompany.co.uk

Just look for the 'free audiobooks' link.

BY THE SAME AUTHOR

DON'T JUST **GIVE** SOMEONE A PALM READING - **LEAVE THEM WITH A SOUVENIR!**

TO BE USED IN CONJUNCTION WITH THE ORIGINAL 'SPEED LEARNING PALMISTRY - PALM READINGS IN YOUR OWN WORDS' BOOK

≈Speed Learning
PALMISTRY
THE SPEED LEARNING PALMISTRY COMPANION SYSTEM

 &

| INSTRUCTION BOOKLET | PALMISTRY CARD 'TICK SHEET' |

A BEAUTIFUL 'GREETINGS CARD' STYLE FORMAT YOUR FRIENDS AND CLIENTS WILL LOVE

Foolproof memory system ~ never miss a thing ~ create a unique momento they'll keep forever!

ADD YOUR DETAILS ~PRINT THEM OUT
SPREAD YOUR NAME!

JULIAN MOORE

INCLUDES GRAPHICS TEMPLATES AND INSTRUCTION MANUAL

BY THE SAME AUTHOR

HOW CAN TEN LETTERS IN TWO WORDS
REVEAL **SO MUCH** ABOUT A PERSON?

≈Speed Learning
GRAPHOLOGY
THE ART OF HANDWRITING ANALYSIS

A fun and easy to use system
you can learn in a weekend

BREAK THE ICE ~
START CONVERSATIONS ~
~ IMPRESS YOUR FRIENDS

"A GREAT WAY TO LEARN THE ART WITHOUT SPENDING HOURS
PLOWING THROUGH THE MANY BOOKS OUT THERE ON THE SUBJECT"
~ RICHARD OSTERLIND

JULIAN MOORE

INCLUDES DOWNLOADABLE AUDIOBOOK AND FLASH CARDS

BY THE SAME AUTHOR

BY THE SAME AUTHOR

24074687R00033

Made in the USA
Lexington, KY
04 July 2013